Our Ancestors
Were Chinese Cranes

Lyrical Poems
by John Freed

Phoenix and Son Press
Portland, OR

2019 Edition

*In order to arrange for poetry readings or
on-site, creative writing workshops*

contact the author

John Freed

Portland, OR

freed@brandman.edu

dedicated to my wife

Stacy Alexander

Prologue

Living in a Japanese House

Your shadow plays
   across the paper screen
   collapsing eyes on moth wings.

From San Diego's Black Beach

Cactus grows leeward.

Naked bodies lie
    random and sexless as birds
    while the ocean's yeasty arms rush my shoes.

Five pelicans ascend with
    the cliff's quick lift
    into the boy's idea of a squadron.

A pair of Navy jets erupts like steam
    from a cappuccino machine
    heading out low over the Pacific.
Wingtips nearly touch like sprinting lovers.

A Review of Freud's Antiquities

Freud's antiquities were on display recently
    at the Blaffer Gallery
    on the campus
    of the University of Houston.

A shirt pocket-sized, cookie cutter cut,
    clay female figure
    of Syrian attribution
    caught my fancy.

Her wide hips, bird face, ambiguous breasts
    and much more practically placed pubis
    seemed the simplest answer
    to all the old man's questions.

Chain of Fools

Graduate school a sonnet doth contain.
Shadows of hands, John Donne and Catullus,
Make you their medium – their succubus –
Charms of belle lettres encircling your chain.

In an Elizabethan garden maze
You go to know what everyone else knows.
"Who wrote 'Lycidas'?" "What's a 'rath primrose'?
Nature is pruned to forbid you your lays.

Esau for his porridge gave up his right;
So look only upon the leaves of pages
That die by foxing, not fall's fiery rages,
Until Keats' colors are black on white.

Then like the day-star rising from the foam,
You'll live eternal on the back of a poem.

Asia   Journal

Kyoto porcelain

Kyoto porcelain
    whirling dervish of coffee cream
    shawls of mountain rain.

Kyoto's Heian Shrine

Is it an antique painting
    of Heian Shrine at
    cherry blossoming
In a gray mountain frame?

Three sharp Shinto
    claps make it so.

A Post-Card from Kyoto at Rush Hour

A perverse quiet even at rush hour
    even from battalions of uniformed teens
    afraid of awakening warlord emperors

At the Pink Bunny Cafe a pastel blue
    elephant stylized into a ball
    wrapped around a raspberry bear

Old women squashed
    into the shape of a Z
    crossing the streets glazed with rain

One thousand and one gold lacquered
    radiantly female images of Kannon
    manifested upright for 733 years

Another wooden temple so vast
    that only rope braided from women's hair
    could have dragged its enormous beams

A glass geometrical monolith
   vaster than Blade Runner's
   imagined future contains

The panther train eager to carry me
   back to Osaka leaving maybe
   a moved pebble at Rengeo-in Zen garden.

Tokyo Grand Kabuki

The kabuki drum
   draws our onnagata
   towards her certain death.

Nara Temple Deer

Quick-eyed deer at Nara Temple
   extort their meals
   from stricken pilgrims.

Taipei Opera School

Charming children
    juggle M'ing bowls with their feet
    for the delight of strangers.

Guilin Karsts

We are drunk
          from snake wine.

Caravans of camel karsts
          float past our tourist boat.

On the Great Wall South of Chengde

On guard now only against
    the sounds of bees
    and mountain winds

I still long for your voice
    like a desolate soldier.

First Emperor's Grave Mound at Xian

It will take much more than 6,000 clay warriors
    and rivers of mercury

To protect the dead emperor
    from his slaughtered people's wrath.

Their heirs won't be bought off by the
    pomegranates and bright orange flowers.

Emperor Mao in Tiananmen Square

Far from that wooden hall
    in polyglot Canton

where he was lean and hard
    as a lightning rod

Mao lies forever a most imperial saint
    sepulchered in his giant's flesh.

Wei Min in Wuhan

Three small leaves
    lay in her ivory hand.

She was the girl again sent down
    some twenty-five years ago
    to work in the North
    on a tea commune.

Ten kilos a day of these
    feather light leaves --
    the smaller the better.

She talked about her three years of pain
    and the life-long misery of the peasants.

Two girls passed us on the dusty road
    arms over shoulders in the Chinese way;
    their legs tied together
    with a red bandanna.

From the Canadian Falls

The Niagara is a human river.

A Japanese man in double-breasted suit
   bends down and slaps a rock.

Purple spiked flowers seem to hold back
   the skeleton of an ore freighter crossways
   not 500 yards from Horseshoe Falls.

"If you wear waterproof mascara, the mist
   won't ruin your face," the mouth's
   ugly beauty chatters while the effluvia of
   the western lakes thunder beneath her legs.

Dates looking more like brothers and sisters
   hold clear plastic bags over their heads.

A Mexican man and wife and all four children
   are dressed in Michael Jordan's #23 jersey.

A woman in a wheel chair digs coins
   from her purse for a small girl
   whose head rests on her lap.

Taking that last snapshot of me forty years ago
   swinging out over the edge, my mother
   melodramatically grabbing at my jacket.

What wasn't shown was her tossing me
   to the rocks hundreds of feet below.

Can you believe that I didn't pop up among
   the debris in the whirlpool at the bend
   in the gorge until just this moment?

Umber Woman

The umber woman's words
      caress me like a sponge

From a tongue
      that flicks out for all those
      black bodies so packed in sweat
      there wasn't air
      enough to speak.

Freed from speech
      their spirits shot up
      to eclipse the sun.

Her words caress me
      like a sponge but
      her tongue flicks out
      between flashing teeth.

She dreamed at long last love

Brought upright
by the sound of glass
she kicked the covers and ran
down the hall toward the light
the love-seat in her office had forced him
into a fetal position
his glasses off his feet bare
he looked too young to be with her
suddenly she was the deer torn
by curiosity and bolting
instead she turned off the desk lamp
took down her mother's afghan
from the top of the bookcase
his face was too close
to her now for her
not to touch it
softer than her own
but with a stubble
she forced herself

to breathe
the afghan snagged
on the settee's carving
she did nothing to free it
she had not caught him that night in her arms
in the morning he would be the one to leave
and she already knew
how much she would hate him for leaving.

He thought of her urgency

He thought of her urgency
the trace of sand on her lips
the kiss's force pushed
back his neck
her caressing hand
intercepted
and properly placed
pitched her forward
onto his chest

he assessed the damage to the beach
an elderly woman wading in the water
with a naked child caught his glance
but would not return it.

Gift of an Anglo Apple

Let me apologize in advance for the English.

It is improper to say, "Please bite apple."
    It must be *my* apple or *this* apple.

As if it were our strictest obligation
    to inventory all creation for a final reckoning.

Not to mention:

Can an Englishman's apple ever be free from
    pesticides, dye, symbol or motive?

How much more suspect then
    should be the language of his love?

Safe for sleep

Safe for sleep
   the mockingbirds scratch
   their way back under the eaves.

Where is your sweet smell?
   A strand of hair keeps me awake.

A butterfly walks

A butterfly walks
   in the monochrome
   of early spring.

Hours are winter nights
   when a lover waits.

Her Mother and Father

Remember the time when you two
   acted just like school-girls
   hanging onto each other's necks,
wearing each other's clothes?

Or that day when you were so small
   that you could ride on her hip,
   your father walking across the park
blackening out the sun?

He would not look you in the eye
   as if the taboo against looking
   could somehow save his sweet Eurydice;
it only left you shadowed by his peasant's back.

But when she dies
   all the air will be squeezed out
   to blow the perfect trumpeter's long
almost breathless sigh.

Your Pen Has Penetrated my Heart

Your pen has penetrated my heart.

Each time that you send a poem,
   I feel myself stripped naked.

How then can your eyes be such mirrors
   as I look for in a friend, when

your pen has penetrated my heart?

(translated from the French)

Scarecrow

for Sylvia Plath

Dad wasn't the Gestapo; he was a POW.

He couldn't eat potato skins
 because that was prison camp food.
 I've only recently begun to eat them myself
 but never without an apologetic tic.

He will receive a check from the VA
 for $45.50 a month for the rest of his life.

Ed Sullivan, himself, interviewed him.
 "Those fucking bastards. . .fucking bastards,"
 he remembered Sullivan answering his own
 dumb question again and again.

The Red Cross sold the skeletons donuts as they
 got off the ship.

A former lover asked me after a year together
 how long you had been dead.
 What a laugh.

You will always be taller than I am,
    but when I was young, more bones than skin
    like my fifteen year old today,

I would suck in my gut and act your starving
    man of war.

You will always be my scarecrow.

"Missing in action presumed dead"
        was all my mother's Christmas in 1944.

I still grieve for our loss.

Waterfowl

I have never made love
   to you the way husbands do,
    more or less on time like an airline.

We have been migrating waterfowl
   feeding along the shore of our
   northern-most lake.

From Jefferson's Monticello

You can actually buy seeds from the gardens
    of Monticello from plants planted by that
    farmer of religious freedom, that inventor of
universities, that multiplier of nations.

Houdin's bust from life watches over the visitors
    shuffling through the large entrance hall,
    people he would have invited in,
had he had the time.

Much of his time was spent bankrupting himself
    paying off his dead wife's dead father's debts
    manufacturing home-grown nails
from imported iron.

He brought a slave to Paris just to learn the
    cooking then the ungrateful man parlayed
    his freedom, one of only seven slaves
freed during his lifetime.

Proud that the sun never caught him
    in that narrow bed nestled in an alcove
    carved directly under the original wall
of his dead love's house,

He spent his life on the painful side of paradise
    believing in an unrisen Christ who left us
    the job of cultivating people
and asparagus in Virginia.

A Love Story in Six Haikai

"Love bade me welcome; yet my soul drew back."

1

Are you that wild
    russet rose
    shy and shameless as a child?

2

Sunset red wildflowers
    guarded by cobwebs
    long to be touched.

3

Variegated carnations
    red and white
    lipstick on the envelop

4

Water spilling from your hands
        fills the vase
        flustered by his violets.

5

Crystal can more lovingly
        hold a stem
        than you hold me in this life.

6

The night wind rises
        soft and strong
        hushing words, lifting trees.

Hungry Owl

What kind father
  leaves his children
  wandering in the woods
  and flies off
  a hungry owl?

Men's Movement

A George Segal papier-mâché man stared
    at the ivory and maroon ripstop
    nylon splayed on the ground.

Then an L. L. Bean man with bandanna kerchief
tied below his Adam's apple and carrying a
huge ceramic mug offered to help.
He was a part-time carpenter from Austin.

Soon two other men stopped by - a former engineer
now psycho-therapist from Oklahoma, and a
journalist from Kansas who I later learned had lost
two small children.

The geodesic tent usually taking me about ten
minutes to set up took the four of us almost an hour.

Over the bush-sized trees, a deep-throated sound
beckoned to the gathering.

And like a herd at dusk to the barn, we silently
    moved toward that sound,
    a drum under each man's arm.

Ishmael

The abandoned son, Ishmael,
    hair flaming out like a dragster's,
    roared and propagated
    to no special purpose
    somewhere in the desert.

Magritte's Le viol

Perfectly polished nails
        violin shaped hair
        down to her waist

Whiter scars across a white throat
        are her silent witnesses.

St. Joan and the Dauphin

Tired of playing the witch,
you held your hands over the fire.

It burned the rope and freed them
then tresses of orange flame
streamed down your face
to garland your hair.

You looked for me somewhere
in dark corners where I was, out of sight.

Your pain was meant to be enough
for the three of us.

Shameless
the fire betrayed your nakedness,
skin and blackened bone.

Finally calm,
you found that gravity
had been in love with you all along.

Finally blessed,
you became lover, mother, son.

Cold Stream

Indifferent to your lovers
    the cold stream smooths
    the black shale

Broken into razors
    by your hiking boots.

From Lake Erie State Park

Lake Erie is that tricolor it gets on windy days
brown near the shore then a band of aqua and
turquoise of the '58 Impala sports sedan
we had before I could drive.

The haze over Canada tints the scene to a perfect
robin's egg
cloudless like my memory of you.

I remember every bit of your round German face
and sky blue eyes. Even the urine smell from the
pavilion is in keeping.

Your power seemed so tenuous like the thousand
razor-thin wires
wound so tightly they could hold up the Brooklyn
Bridge.

They held you up; they held me up.
The tension snapped you in two
and brought me here alone.

My wife may be back at Heart's Content in the
Allegheny Forest where she and her lover
had a matchless time.

If I asked her, she would tell me.
But dreading Othello's too small cage,
I am sufficiently satisfied not knowing.

Satisfied making out your sky blue eyes
in the October blue's skies.

Hurricanoes

Cats seek shelter under
        broken asbestos tiles
        speakers blown in their ears
        by sheets of lightning.

Sitting naked on the lawn,
        I neither hear nor feel
        the side-swiping hurricane.

It appears as TV background noise
        for more domestic violence.

My arms across your shoulders

My arms across your shoulders
      holding your hands apart
      the shard of glass from your wrist

Sculpted by Bernini
      into a world of our own.

From Ferguson Point Teahouse
Vancouver, British Columbia

I've escaped to an inner-city, wilderness peninsula
where I'm writing on a carpet of maple leaves as big
as baskets.

Nine enormous ships rest directly in front; green
mountains rise from the ocean on the right, and a
tall blonde in a lemon slicker has just jogged by
smiling to nobody in particular.

The question is, should I hurry to catch a ferry
before Vancouver's rush-hour back to my stale
conference in Seattle, or should I for once in my life
just stay where I hate to leave?

"I'm going to walk back to the Ferguson Point
Teahouse," I'm actually saying the words out loud
like a crazy person.

A single carnation, pale yellow piped with
raspberry, brushes the window with its face. I flirt
with the Steak and Kidney Pie but choose the
Oriental Chicken Salad as if foreordained.

Catching the end of a conversation at the next table between a man and a woman whose dress matches her lipstick, I think I hear him say, "I love you more than I don't dislike my wife."

Outside again along the water-walk in the painfully bright cold I pass two older Eastern European sounding men.

"I'm not going to spoil you by giving you 10,000," the older, older protests.

"Then when are you going to buy me a trip to Europe or Hawaii?"

Canada seems no longer willing or able to offer asylum, either sexual or political, at least not just across the border.

Shiva's Imminence

Smelling of burnt grass
        your hair hides dark water eyes.

I worship nothing so much
        as the liquid in those eyes.

Faces are metaphors too.
        I love her because of you.

Wyatt's Deer

Two deer woke me
          stalking my open tent.

They were small, young or female,
          a little reckless, alert.

A brown wood thrush hopped.

The deer started, then froze,
     like perfect breasts in that photograph of you.

I should have raced with you out of grace
          your hair gone wild
          caught by the fairy wind
the accelerating instant before the crash.

From the Piazza da Mill Valley

Halloween's late morning produces
more toddlers in pumpkins holding still for their
mothers' camcorders than real memories,

more dogs testy over scraps of croissants,

a white children's costume parade accompanied by a
fire engine straight out of a Golden Book,

dreamsicle woman nursing a latte in glasses
a strand of hair alarms her as if it were a bug,

new age father -- more colorfully decorated than his
child --letting it loose among the dogs' noses,

a tailored dyke with sensationally thick buzz
cropped blonde hair,

teenaged retro-hippies barefoot, exotic in slit harem
pants and filthy striped bells, faces round
and delicate only because they're young
permitting the homeless man to squat on the fringes
of their circle,

a police officer concerned that the real street person
remains awake and gets his free large orange juice,

high body images legs skin-tight, tip-toeing on
cleated shoes, bicycles costing more than my old
Saab laid on their sides to sun like seals,

in the mini version of a Catholic school girl's pleated
plaid skirt a photographer silently firing her Leica at
the hippie lovers making out ambiguously sexual
only in their dress,

a native skinned American, looking as if he should
be in school, dressed in dark blue sweats juggling a
soccer ball in slow motion with his feet.

Energy emanates from a small child careening over
the brick work, a black and gold Tinkerbell with
green aluminum wand,

and from a petite business woman carrying a huge
manila envelope clicking onto the street
to wave down the town's only cab.

She reminds me of Carla who once turned
translucent for me.

I'm sure she is a grown up business woman now
who wears Armani on the last day of October
in Mill Valley, California.

Like a cowboy lover

Like a cowboy lover,
     more prick than sense,
     the black metal dog
     springs toward a brown metal barrel
     through a wire capital O
     dropping his coin
     somewhere short of the mark.

The truth is

Confidently we undress.

But the truth is
we more often act like Jews
in a pogrom
fleeing from each other
than we act like lovers.

More terrified of our power together
        than of our separate deaths.

On the Oregon Coast

Pushing through the damp sand
      head low past the sign,
        "Lab on the loose, Drive Slow,"

She doesn't see the rock shaped head
      bobbing as if exhausted
      too far out to sea.

An Ode to James Merrill:
A Regret

I've never been gay but late in
      life I regret not
      being sucked by one of the
      most important poets
      in America.

We met one night in
      the apartment of his
      acolyte – my lover.

He, more boyish the
      older he became.
I, more regretful
      of worm holes I'd
      never explore.

I can hear his clarinet
      voice still in
      "The owlet umlaut peeps
      and hoots
      above the open vowel."

Mine, I'm certain evaporated
    like the
    the buzzing of a bee.

James Merrill listening to me.

Photo courtesy of Judith Moffett

In Your Skin
for Judith Moffett

I can imagine what it's like to live
    in your skin, my loving friend.

Brilliant words protruding from your belly
    like poems sent from a Salem witch.

A smooth, wooden phallus carved in his shape
    pumps your heart.

A fetus rolls safely, closely
    in your darkness – still smelling of us.

Our breasts, shrunken by losses,
    leak milk and blood.

And I expel my breath
    out through your mouth.

And we are whole and young again,
    your kidneys resting in my cupped hands.

Judas' Gospel

Judas scaled the cedar fence last night
       to ruminate among
         my pea green pecans.

Selfless

His last mortal thought
       was the starburst green
       a bottle of Heineken makes
       hitting black asphalt.

Why would a nineteen year old
       jump off a cliff in Austin, Texas?

Nothing human would find him
       for eighty-one more days.

Ars gratia sanguis

The small palette knife
        slashes his painted
        head into halves.

Sangria splatters the walls.

Living with Mice

I confess. My house is infested with mice
      No matter where I live.
Flashing across the baseboards
      Upsetting my rest like sin.

The mice never scratch for forgiveness.
      They just don't care.
They are what they are
      And aren't what they are not.

I once heard a person proudly say
      she was living with a homeless woman.
They sounded like mice to me,
      and I envied their loving carelessness.

Last Christmas in Galveston

My last Christmas covered by a scrim of fog
        distant houses forming chalky cliffs.

The Gulf's shaming surf punctuated
        by quizzical bursts of gull shrieks.

A bleached snake skull crunched
        under foot like a glass ornament.

How warm the water still was
        with what a shrimp-boil taste.

Nobody's dog ran up the beach
        barking at me like a lifeguard.

Even the waves pushed me back
        insisting I was earth and meant for dust.

Amber

My heart's altar, it turns out,
      is not so much marble as amber,

That honey golden resin
      preserving nettlesome insects
      in such a semi-precious way.

Epilogue

Pittsburgh's Northside

The old carpenter
          planing window sash
          was   not   there.

Made in the USA
Columbia, SC
20 April 2019